The Tower of London: The History of England's Famous Landmark

By Dr. Jesse Harasta and Charles River Editors

Bob Collowân's picture of the Tower of London

About Charles River Editors

Charles River Editors provides superior editing and original writing services across the digital publishing industry, with the expertise to create digital content for publishers across a vast range of subject matter. In addition to providing original digital content for third party publishers, we also republish civilization's greatest literary works, bringing them to new generations of readers via ebooks.

Introduction

Picture of the original entrance to the White Tower

The Tower of London

The Tower of London is one of the most historic sites in all of England, and still one of the most popular. All around is the modern City of London, one of the world's most prosperous and power financial districts, but the Tower is still a daunting structure that looms across the landscape. Not a single structure but a vast network of medieval and early modern fortifications, it anchors the southeastern end of the old City and controls access to the River Thames and, through it, London's connection to the sea. While the both the City and the Thames are often obscured by the walls once visitors are inside the Tower, they are inextricably tied to the building, giving the Tower its entire reason for existence.

Even today, taking a tour of the Tower can seemingly bring its history to life. Inside the visitor center are replicas of a crown, an executioner's axe and similar artifacts, but for most visitors, this is just the start. After they cross a small courtyard and approach the first gate, known as the Middle Tower, they come to a stone bridge over a now-dry moat and enter the castle itself through the Byward Tower. The Tower, like many fortresses of its day, was built in concentric rings, so inside the outer wall is a narrow strip of land before the inner walls. Long, narrow buildings line the inside of the outer wall, and to the left along Mint Street these structures once housed the operation of the Royal Mint, making all of the coins of the realm.

From there, most visitors continue straight along, typically guided by one of the colorfully-dressed Yeoman Guards (the famous "Beefeaters"). Under the watch of the Bell Tower, they continue along the south face of the inner wall, on Water Lane, and just ahead is the famed Traitor's Gate; while today the area around here is paved and dry, in earlier times this was a "watergate" that allowed boats entry to the fortress. It was so named because this was the entrance by which prisoners (often traitors) entered the fortress, often never to leave. Ahead is Wakefield Tower, the entrance to the inner courtyards and a space that can be rented for small banquets and private dinners.

Inside the inner courtyards, visitors get a good first look at the White Tower, the 11th century Norman castle at the heart of the Tower (and the original "Tower" the entire complex is named for). Built of distinctive white stone, it has been a beacon of royal power for centuries. It is four stories tall and at points has walls of up to 15 feet thick, with towers on the four corners that have cupolas atop them (added much later than the original structure). Within the Tower is an impressive collection of medieval armor and arms, as well as the well-preserved St. John's Chapel. Directly behind the White Tower is the Waterloo Block, also known as the Jewel House. A perennial favorite of visitors, the Crown Jewels of the United Kingdom are stored here when not in use.

In the southeast corner of the inner courtyard (the "Inner Ward") is a charming green space backed by lovely Tudor structures whose calm belies their bloody history. This is the Tower Green which was the location of the executions of all of those prisoners who were given "Private" deaths (as opposed to a "Public" death which occurred outside the walls on Tower Hill before the London mob). It is perhaps best known as the site of the deaths of three of Henry VIII's wives: Anne Boleyn, Catherine Howard, and Jane Grey. One of the surrounding buildings, the Queen's House, was named after its most famous prisoner - Anne Boleyn - but was also the site of the trial of the notorious Guy Fawkes.

Other sites within the walls of the Tower include the famous ravens (according to legend, if they ever leave the Tower the monarchy will fall), the museum of the Royal Regiment of

Fusiliers (whose ceremonial commander is the Constable of the Tower) and the Ceremony of the Keys. The Ceremony is performed nightly by the Yeoman Warders when they seal the gates of the Tower and the Chief Warder passes the keys to the Resident Governor. Just beyond the Tower rises the great supports of the Tower Bridge (often confused with the smaller London Bridge) and the Thames.

Ultimately, it's impossible to fully appreciate the Tower without understanding its context. Like all fortresses, it was built to control and protect its surroundings, and the history of the Tower is bound up in the mutual histories of London and the Monarchy. The unfolding saga of war, imprisonment, glory, and treason in England can all be told through the lens of the Tower, and the lives that intersected with it.

The Tower of London: The History of England's Famous Landmark looks at the history of the Tower from the Middle Ages to today. Along with pictures of important people, places, and events, you will learn about the Tower of London like never before, in no time at all.

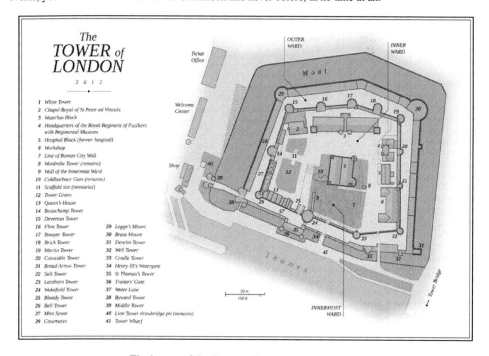

The layout of the Tower of London today

Chapter 1: Origins of the Tower

The story of the Tower of London begins in 1066, when the Duke of Normandy, William, landed at Pevensy in the south and marched to Hastings, where he defeated his rival, the Saxon king Harold, ending seven centuries of rule by the Germanic Saxon royal families. Looking back historically, this victory on the field of battle clinched the Norman Conquest, but it was not so obvious to those on the ground at the time. In fact, the Saxon elite chose a new king, Edgar, who rallied Saxon resistance, requiring William to march up the Thames until he reached the city of Southwark, which faced London across the river. Here, the Saxons actually won a victory, defending the London Bridge and the city itself. Knowing that London was the key to the kingdom, William marched east to a crossing and then headed back towards the capital. Edgar had been unable to raise a sufficient army to drive out the Normans, so when William arrived at the city gates, London surrendered and William was crowned in Westminster Abbey. William consolidated his rule and then returned to Normandy, henceforth known to history as William the Conqueror[1].

William and his half-brothers depicted in the Bayeux Tapestry

William the Conqueror is remembered for being the last foreign invader to conquer the island, but even then, the picture was not so simple, because the Saxons deeply resented Norman control and began rebellions in 1067, 1069, 1071 and 1075. Moreover, Harold's sons took control of Dublin and launched raids along the west coast of England for many years. The Normans

---

1   "Essential Norman Conquest" by Osprey Publishing. Accessed online at:
    http://www.essentialnormanconquest.com/

gradually consolidated their control over the new kingdom primarily through the construction of a series of elaborate, expensive fortifications. These castles did have the purpose of protecting England from outside assault (such as from the always troublesome Danes or the sons of Harold), but they were far more important for their ability to serve as points of control for dominating the English landscape and people, and the single most important fortification constructed during this period was the Tower of London, undoubtedly inspired by William's insights into the importance of that city for his campaign of 1066.

William's original tower was built for supremely practical reasons, as it represented the Normans' attempt to control the city of London. London has long served as the commercial hub of England, in large part because of the existence of the London Bridge, the only crossing of the River Thames for the majority of its length, and the Tower was positioned downriver from the Bridge, just within the Roman fortifications of the city[2]. Before the construction of the great ports of East London, all river traffic (and hence all traffic from the sea) had to pass up past the Tower into the Upper Pool where it was unloaded into the city. As a result, the Tower could benefit from (and strengthen) the existing fortifications of the city, control the routes of trade and potential invasion of the city by foreign powers, and serve as a social control over the city residents themselves.

Rafa Esteve's picture of the Tower of London and its position on the Thames

The relationship between the City of London and the Crown has been a complex one for now

---

2   "London Bridge" in The Encyclopedia Britannica. Accessed online at:
    http://www.britannica.com/EBchecked/topic/347007/London-Bridge

close to a thousand years, and when William arrived in London, he found a form of governance that was rooted in the time of the Roman Empire. Across the Empire, as the Romans colonized, they formed semi-autonomous local municipal governments based upon the Ancient Greek model, but when the Empire collapsed, these cities gained some semblance of independence. Though most of those in the Western Empire fell in the subsequent years, London retained its own government, which had not been created but instead simply recognized by the Saxon Kings[3].

William continued this relationship by "recognizing" the City with a charter, thereby giving his blessing to an institution that he did not control. To this day, the City of London (which is a single square mile around the financial district and St. Paul's Cathedral) is a unique administrative unit within the United Kingdom, where the laws of the UK (especially in regards to financial matters) do not completely apply. Today, this is primarily a mechanism by which "City" bankers subvert attempts to regulate their industry, but in the medieval period, this was a powerful check on royal authority in the region and a necessary evil for the Normans, who relied upon the City's economic weight to bolster their rule[4].

However they might have needed the City, William and his heirs did not fully trust it, and the creation of the Tower of London is only the most obvious marker of their desire to assert royal authority over the troublesome City and make sure that it primarily served royal needs, not its own. Of course, this control was never complete, but the subsequent history of the Tower is closely tied to the history of the city as it slowly rose to become a massive metropolis and the center of a global empire.

---

3 "London" in The Encyclopedia Britannica. Accessed online at:
   http://www.britannica.com/EBchecked/topic/346821/London
4 "The Tax Haven in the Heart of Britain" by Nicholas Shaxson in *New Statesman* 24 February 2011

Bernard Gagnon's picture of the White Tower, the original structure

The Tower was not unique in this role as a multi-faceted expression of control. As archaeologist Matthew Johnson pointed out in his study of Bodiam Castle along the southeast coast of England, castles were traditionally seen as part of a wider national attempt to defend England from potential foreign invaders mimicking the Norman Conquest of 1066. Thus, Bodiam Castle was located along the River Rother, at the point where it was no longer easily navigable, making it the furthest spot upriver where an invasion fleet could disembark. Johnson's analysis has shown, however, that the Castle had more than this national defense role, as it was also designed to control a chokepoint in the movement of people and goods across the landscape. This checkpoint was an easy ford of the river, where food and wool and other goods crossed the water. In this way, the lord of the castle was able to exert political and economic control over the countryside without necessarily having to have his agents in every village and hearth of the hills[5].

---

5   "Understanding Bodiam: Landscapes Of Work At A Late Medieval English Castle" talk by Matthew Johnson given at Syracuse University. March 6th, 2014, 4pm.

The difference is that Bodiam Castle was a relatively small fortification located in a relatively marginal area of Britain, and its owner was a minor member of the nobility. The Tower, on the other hand, was a massive, carefully constructed military center which dominated the most important city and the most important river on the isle of Britain. Through the control over trade in London – on the Thames and on the London Bridge – the monarchy was able to assert its power over the economic life of the entire nation. While the Tower does not physically do this today since the shipping no longer passes beneath its crenellations, symbolically it still serves this role, asserting the ultimate authority of the British Monarchy and hence the State over the myriad financial transactions of the City of London's firms and their global reach. Of course, just like in the days of William, this control was never perfect or complete.[6]

The original Norman castle is today known as the White Tower. The current structure - expanded several times since - is constructed of stone and replaced the first fortification here: a timber fort raised up quickly after the Conquest. Work probably began in the late 1070s, and it was definitely done by the 1100s. The construction was a massive undertaking for the time, and the *Anglo-Saxon Chronicle* notes that "many shires whose labour was due to London were hard pressed because of the wall that they built around the Tower". The final building was easily the most impressive fortification in Britain: a square 36 meters by 32.5 meters and 27.5 meters tall at its greatest point. It was integrated into the Roman walls of the city (and was the first truly great piece of military architecture in Britain since their time), and it was further guarded by its own system of moats and dikes.[7]

6   "Tower of London" in the *Encyclopedia Britannica*. Accessed online at: Tower of London (tower, London, United Kingdom)
7   "Norman Beginnings" in the *Historic Royal Palaces: Tower of London* website. Accessed online at: http://www.hrp.org.uk/TowerOfLondon/sightsandstories/buildinghistory/normanbeginnings#sthash.HHnaqozK.d puf

A medieval illustration of the White Tower

Michael Wal's picture of a suit of armor used by King Henry VIII now displayed in the White Tower

For William and his immediate descendants, the White Tower served a number of practical purposes. In addition to the defense of London from outside attack and control over the flows of goods, people and money through the City and its environs, the Tower was also home to numerous elements of the royal bureaucracy. It was, of course, home to the king during his time in the City, though it never rivaled the importance or opulence of the Palace of Westminster several miles upriver. Famously, it was also the only regular royal prison, and as such it housed numerous prisoners, famous and forgotten over the centuries. It was also at different times the location of the royal armory, treasury and even menagerie for the royal court.

While the White Tower was remarkable for its size and must have been awe-inspiring for the population of London and travelers at the time, including pilgrims and merchants passing through London, it was not particularly remarkable for its design. When the Normans arrived in Britain, they brought with them a relatively sophisticated understanding of military engineering and a well-established plan for the creation of their strongholds. The White Tower is just one of many similar structures, now fittingly called "Norman Keeps", that dotted the post-Invasion British landscape. Similar buildings can still be found in Rochester, Newcastle, Dover, Brough, Norwich, Guilford, Appleby, Castle Rising, Colchester and elsewhere.

The typical Norman Keep was a square structure, much taller than it was wide, with square towers rising above the main structures and protruding outwards from the main wall at each corner. Unlike the stereotypical castle of public memory, these keeps often did not have curtain walls (outer walls enclosing a courtyard), though the White Tower did, but stood alone on the landscape. The Keep served as living quarters for the noble owner, as well as a banquet hall, storage, living quarters for soldiers and servants, storage, and a chapel for the inhabitants.[8]

Panorama of the curtain walls

8   "Norman Square Keeps" accessed online at TimeRef. Available at: TimeRef - Medieval and Middle Ages History Timelines - Episodes of Medieval History

Bernard Gagnon's picture of St. John's Chapel inside the White Tower

In many ways, the White Tower is prototypical of this design, as it was built upon an ideal location, the flat lands around the Thames Valley, so its builders did not need to make any accommodations for topography. In addition to its size, the other major difference of the White Tower from the traditional design was a round tower on the northeast corner and an enlarged rounded-edge tower on the southeast corner. The building's designer was Gundulf of Rochester, a monk who crossed the Channel soon after the Norman invasion and was eventually appointed in 1075 as the Bishop of Rochester. Known as a military engineer, he would eventually supervise the construction of not only the White Tower but similar strongholds in Rochester and Colchester. Rochester Castle in particular takes the classic Norman Keep form and was built to control both the road from Rochester to London and the crossing of the River Medway (much as the White Tower controls the crossing of the Thames). Today, Gundulf is still known as the "Father of the Corps of Royal Engineers."[9]

9   "Rochester Castle" at the webpage of English Heritage, accessed online at: http://www.english-heritage.org.uk/daysout/properties/rochester-castle/

Chapter 2: Norman Stronghold until the Anarchy

After the Norman Conquest, England and the Tower enjoyed only two generations of relative peace under the Norman Dynasty of William's heirs. The Tower was completed in 1079, and when William died in 1087 and was succeeded by his son, William Rufus, repairs were made for storm damage at the tower in 1091. The city during this period was mostly contained within the 326 acres enclosed by the Roman walls and home to between 30,000 and 40,000 inhabitants. It was a bustling place at the confluence of all of the major (Roman era) roads of the island, where influences, people and goods from across Britain and beyond converged. The homes were almost entirely made of wood and were only a few stories at most, making the great stone tower the most impressive structure in the City.[10]

The Norman overlords had consolidated their power during William's reign and ruled over a relatively peaceful and prosperous island. The first was William Rufus, who reigned from 1087 until 1100, and then his younger brother Henry I from 1100 to 1135 after William Rufus died in a hunting accident. After Henry's son and heir William died in the sinking of his ship, *The White Ship*, in 1120, the succession was put into doubt. His death from sickness in 1135 led to a crisis of succession and, then, into a bloody civil war. This war is known in history as "The Anarchy" and was fought between Stephen of Blois and the Empress Matilda. Stephen was the grandson of William the Conqueror through his mother, while Matilda was the daughter of Henry I. The Anarchy raged until 1154 and was not simply a war between two royal factions but a complete breakdown of law and order throughout England.

---

10 Hibbert 1971 21-23

A medieval illustration depicting Empress Matilda

Meanwhile, superb Norman military engineering in fortifications like the Tower of London had greatly outstripped the technology of siege engines, meaning that each side was able to hold onto its strongholds for extended periods and the enemy had to resort to prolonged sieges. Most of the war thus consisted of roving warrior bands associated with one faction or the other leaving their places of strength and ravaging the countryside around enemy strongholds, with the hope of depriving them of needed supplies. This, of course, was devastating for the countryside.

At times, the Tower seemed the only shelter in a storm of violence and danger. For most of the war, Stephen controlled London and the Tower – at first with support of the mob of London (a force of great power within the national politics), but at a later period in the war, he lost that support and was forced to retreat into the Tower while the citizenry besieged it[11]. In 1141, Matilda's forces temporarily defeated Stephen, and the Constable of the Tower - Geoffrey de Mandeville II - surrendered the stronghold to Matilda in return for forgiving the harsh fines imposed upon his father, the first Constable, for allowing Bishop Flambard to escape in 1101. Matilda arrived in the Tower, but when she attempted to have a coronation, the London mob drove her back and forced her to take refuge in the Tower. Eventually, she lost control of it again, and from that point forward she slowly lost the war.

This period also begins the tradition of using the Tower as a prison. The first prisoner held within its walls was Bishop Ranulf Flambard, who had served as the chief tax collector for King William Rufus. The taxes had been considered exorbitant, and the new king, Henry I, accused Ranulf Flambard of corruption and had him imprisoned in 1101. This was hardly a difficult sentence, however, since he had been in the Tower for barely six months before he staged a brazen escape. He threw a banquet (this was the extent of his freedom within the Tower) and got his guards drunk, and then escaped through a window in a rope smuggled in a wine jug. His allies were waiting at the foot of the Tower, and they escaped into the night. He would eventually ally with Henry's older brother, the Duke of Normandy, and aid him in a failed invasion of England before retiring from public life[12].

In many ways Bishop Flambard's time in the Tower was typical of the age. He was a powerful prisoner whose "crimes" consisted primarily of joining the wrong side in a political duel, but he remained influential enough to avoid execution. These individuals led lives of relative splendor in the Tower and still enjoyed most of the benefits of their rank.

However, there was a darker side to imprisonment that would emerge after Flambard's time: torture and execution. Today, the Tower's tortures and executions – and resulting tales of ghosts – are a source of both repulsion and grisly fascination for visitors and scholars alike. That said, to understand this role of the Tower, it's necessary to understand the mentality of the medieval torturer and executioner. French theorist Michel Foucault has written extensively on this topic, and he noted, "One no longer touched the body [in modern punishments], or at least as little as possible, and then only to reach something other than the body..." Thus, the torture was "an instrument, an intermediary" through which the punishing government attempted to manipulate the freedom, the spirit or the soul of the incarcerated. At the same time, this process was removed from the realm of public spectacle, which so often accompanied medieval torture[13]. Later, Foucault notes that the tortures of the Tower and elsewhere in Europe were "not an extreme expression of lawless rage" but instead a calculated application of a studied pain which is designed to carefully crescendo to the moment when the body ceases to live but can (and

---

11 Hibbert 30
12 "Ranulf Flambard" in the *Historic Royal Palaces: Tower of London* website. Accessed online at:
     http://www.hrp.org.uk/learninganddiscovery/Discoverthehistoricroyalpalaces/Prisoners/RanulfFlambard
13 *Discipline and Punish: Birth of the Prison* by Michel Foucault (1995). Pg 11

frequently did) continue long after physical death.

A torture device on display in the Tower

The public nature of the death was part of the process: "the fact that the guilty man should moan and cry out under the blows is not a shameful side-effect, it is the very ceremonial of justice being expressed in all its force… justice pursues the body beyond all possible pain." This was not for the purpose of reforming the offender but instead forcibly removing the stain of the crime upon the community of the state through the application of excessive violence[14].

---

14 *Ibid* pgs 33 - 34

This context, where royal rule was reinforced and reinstated after insurrection or crime through the complete annihilation of the offender, is crucial for understanding the Tower. Within the Tower, this type of torture and punishment did occur, but most frequently, these punishments occurred elsewhere, specifically the prison of Newgate and the gallows on Tyburn Hill. Instead, the Tower was the site of a different form of punishment from the norm. Most of the Tower executions occurred in "private" (within the courtyard and not in public spectacle) and were of the swift and – for the time – humane method of a single blow by a blade from the executioner without torture.

In fact, the executions in the Tower were not just abnormal but quite rare; only 22 people have been put to death in the Tower, compared to thousands at Tyburn. This is because they were not public spectacles or rituals of royal power, but instead tended to be more secretive events meant to eliminate political rivals or troublesome wives (in the case of Henry VIII) whose more open execution could be events for public outcry. These "private" executions were also considered to be more respectful and appropriate for those who the monarch felt should maintain some sense of decency.

Chris Nyborg's photo of the site of the scaffold

Chapter 3: The Tower During the Plantagenet Dynasty

Peace returned to England in the summer of 1153 when the son of Matilda, Henry, signed a treaty with Stephen and was recognized as Stephen's heir. When Stephen died the following year, Henry II was crowned and the process of rebuilding began. Work began on the Tower in 1155, when Thomas Becket, at that point Archdeacon of Canterbury, Lord Chancellor of the Realm, was also made Keeper of the Works at the Tower. Becket would eventually be appointed Archbishop of Canterbury and would then be martyred on the grounds of Canterbury Cathedral by the King's men when he refused to accede to the Constitutions of Clarendon, a law which put the Church under the crown. Today he is recognized as St. Thomas Becket for his sacrifice and holiness.

A medieval depiction of Henry II and Thomas Becket

The Tower entered a quiet period after these repairs until the reign of Richard I, "the Lionheart" (1189 -1199). The son of Henry II, Richard began a project of impressive expansion before leaving to fight the Third Crusade in 1190. Richard left the Tower and England under the hands of his Lord Chancellor William Longchamp, the Bishop of Ely. Longchamp, realizing the precariousness of his position without his patron, quickly finished the Tower expansions. As knights refused to recognized Longchamp and turned to support Richard's brother, John, Longchamp attempted to besiege their castles, sparking a small-scale civil war that ended up with Longchamp besieged within the Tower of London. Eventually, the Tower fell to John, and though Longchamp escaped, John took the throne and held it until Richard's return.15

15 "The Medieval Tower" in the *Historic Royal Palaces: Tower of London* website. Accessed online at:
http://www.hrp.org.uk/TowerOfLondon/sightsandstories/buildinghistory/medievalTower

The funeral effigy of Richard the Lionheart

After Richard's return, he eventually named John his successor. John I took the throne in 1199 and was frequently a guest at the Tower. In fact, it is believed that he was the first king to bring exotic animals, including lions, to live at the Tower, but in 1215, at the start of the next civil war (the First Barons' War), John's opponents seized the Tower as one of their first acts. The king died in 1216, and his nine-year old son, Henry III took the throne, eventually defeating the Barons.

Henry III was a remarkably long-lived and long-reigning king, holding the throne from 1216 until 1272, but the king's supporters - fearful of more revolt - realized the weaknesses in the Tower's defenses and in the 1220s expanded the fortress, adding the Wakefield and Lanthorn towers along the riverfront, ostensibly as lodging for the king and queen respectively. In 1238, there was another smaller uprising of the Barons, and the king fled to the Tower, during which he observed weaknesses in its defenses and began yet another building project. The king had massive walls, a watery moat and nine additional towers added on all of the Tower's landward sides. This was a time of uncertainty and fear and many London residents, seeing the ever-expanding Tower as a symbol of royal oppression, rejoiced when part of the walls and a tower near the Beauchamp Tower collapsed. Some attributed the event to the people's patron against royal excesses: St. Thomas Becket[16].

---

16 *Ibid*

A panorama with Wakefield Tower to the left and the White Tower to the right

Dirk Ingo Franke's picture of the former location of the moat

An amusing side note from this period was the 1251 arrival of a polar bear in the Tower. The walls of the fortress had become home to the royal menagerie, a proto-zoo for the enjoyment and prestige of the court, and since these bears had to be imported from the Norse colony of Greenland, they served as "spectacular status symbols" in the royal courts of Europe. The Norse hunters had to capture the bear alive without tranquilizers or firearms, tie it up, and bring it for weeks on their tiny boats down first to their settlements and then over the high seas to Europe. Given those difficulties, the presence of such a creature at the Tower of London demonstrated the immense prestige given to this particular fortification in the eyes of the monarchy[17].

In 1263, all of the tensions and fears broke out into the Second Barons' War which lasted until 1267. The baron Simon de Montfort rallied dissatisfied barons against the king and in 1263 rapidly captured much of southeast England. Henry and his son Edward I ("Longshanks") retreated to the Tower but were besieged their and eventually surrendered and were captured by Simon. In 1265, Edward escaped and rallied the royalists to his side, slowly beating back Simon and recapturing the Tower.

Bernard Gagnon's picture of a replica of Edward I's bedchambers in the Tower

Like his father, when Edward I came to power, he also went on a campaign of expanding the

17 *Collapse: How Societies Choose to Fail or Succeed* by Jared Diamond (2005). Viking Books. Pgs 240 - 243

Tower's defenses, recognizing its crucial role in any uprising. Thus, between 1275 and 1279, he turned his attention to the river-side defenses, and St. Thomas' Tower and the Traitor's Gate (a water gate where boats can enter the fortress) were created. Also during this period (1279 specifically) there is the first mention of the cost of buildings to house the Royal Mint within the Tower[18]. Edward also began the tradition of housing royal valuables in the Tower, creating a branch of the Royal Mint there and keeping much of his treasure safely out of the hands of his enemies and in its vaults.

A model of the expansion of the Tower conducted under Edward I

His son, Edward II (who ruled from 1307-1327), retreated to the Tower and lived there more-or-less permanently in response to regular uprisings by barons unhappy with his reign, but Edward II's son reversed the weakness of his father's reign and waged war on Scotland and France. In 1360, the Tower became the home of John II ("The Good"), the king of France, who lived there in splendor during his imprisonment. Finally, in the reign of Richard II, the kingdom was convulsed by the Peasants Revolt and the Tower was stormed by the mob of London, which captured and executed Simon of Sudbury, the Archbishop of Canterbury, in 1381. After the end of the rebellion, there were further repairs and expansions, including the Tower Wharf, which was supervised by Geoffrey Chaucer, the Clerk of Works in 1389 (and later author of *The Canterbury Tales*). Parallel to these internal threats was the ongoing brutality of the Hundred

---

18 "Royal Mint Timeline" at the Homepage of the *Museum of the Royal Mint*. Accessed online at:
   http://www.royalmintmuseum.org.uk/history/timeline/index.html

Years War (1337 - 1453), which was fought primarily in today's France but in which the Tower was also considered to be a part of a larger system of national defense.

In essence, with the exception of the White Tower, the Tower of London came to take its modern form largely during the troubled reigns of Richard I, Henry III and Edward I. The sprawling stronghold was a product of the military technology and propaganda demands of the time and is as much a symbol of royal instability in the late 1100s and throughout the 1300s as it is of royal power in the era. This was a period when England was drawn into a wider arena of European royal politics; under the Saxons, the island had been at first completely aloof from the larger European events, but after 1066, it was integrated into a larger state that included substantial holdings in France. Hence, the Tower was part of a much larger network of fortifications throughout England, Wales, Ireland[19], and northern and western France, typical of the military style of the time and remarkable more for its size than uniqueness.

Chapter 4: The Tudors

The Tudors would rule England and its other territories from 1485-1603, but their kingdom was very different from that of the Normans and previous dynasties. Since it included no French lands, the Tudors were almost entirely focused upon England and the British Isles. By losing their continental lands in the Hundred Years War, the rulers of England had in essence become "English" again, and in the process London became the administrative, economic and military center of the state. In conjunction with that, the great fortress of the Tower was no longer one (albeit large) part of a vast network of fortifications but instead the beating heart of royal military power.

While the Norman period involved numerous military upsets and periods of violence, the first prolonged civil war since the Anarchy occurred in 1455 and lasted until 1487. Known as the Wars of the Roses, it pit the House of York against the House of Lancaster, both of which traced their ancestry back to William the Conqueror, and as in previous wars, the Tower remained a point of central concern for both parties. The upper hand passed back and forth between the two, and in 1471, the Yorkists held the Tower and used it to first imprison and then execute Henry VI, the Lancastrian king and great-grandson of Richard II. In this act, the House of Lancaster was extinguished by the Yorkists, but their cause was taken up by the House of Tudor from Wales. During the War, the Tower served as a place of not only control but also celebration, most notably as a safe place to hold the coronation of Edward IV.

---

19 Dublin Castle, for example, was built after 1204 on the orders of John I - consolidating his family's conquest of 1169. It was probably the most far-flung of such castles.

Portrait of Henry VI

Richard Nevell's picture of the room in the Wakefield Tower where Henry VI died

During these conflicts, both sides imprisoned their enemies in the Tower when they held control of it, and perhaps the most famous prisoner of the era was Sir Thomas Malory, an apparent Yorkist rogue who was accused of ambushing the Lancastrian Duke of Buckingham and of seducing the wives of Lancastrian noblemen. While imprisoned in the tower before his death in 1471, he took the time to pen *Le Morte d'Arthur*, the first major compilation of the tales of King Arthur. It is likely that as a prisoner, he had access to an excellent library that he drew upon in the Tower, as well as the time and resources with which to write.

This was also the period of one of the most haunting stories of the Tower: the Princes in the Tower. The two boys, Edward and Richard, were the sons of the Yorkist King Edward IV (who had captured and executed Henry VI), and like previous kings, Edward IV had stored his most precious "treasures" in the Tower during times of danger, in this case his two sons and heirs. When the boys were 12 and 9, respectively, their father died, perhaps of typhoid fever but also possibly of poison. The King named his brother - Richard - the Lord Protector of the kingdom and guardian of his two sons. Soon after, young Edward - today considered Edward V despite never being crowned - and his brother disappeared from the public eye. Their uncle, Richard III, took the throne in 1483 and has been often accused by historians of killing the two, though there are several other suspects.

John Everett Millais' painting, "The Two Princes in the Tower"

Two years later, in 1485, Richard III fell on the field of battle at Bosworth while fighting against Henry Tudor, who became the king of the new dynasty, and some insisted that the loss of faith in his rule due to his apparent murder of his nephews weakened Richard's Yorkist side. Nonetheless, the princes' disappearance continued to haunt the Tudors for some time after, especially when a lad named Lambert Simnel was said to be the young prince Richard by a group of Yorkists in 1487. Under the basis of Simnel's legitimacy, they attempted to revolt against Henry Tudor, and from 1491-1497, another supposed Richard, a man named Perkin Warbeck, attacked the western territories, costing the Tudor state a considerable amount in wealth, attention and military power.

To prevent similar occurrences, Henry Tudor, who became Henry VII, took the throne in 1485 and married Elizabeth of York, the older sister of the two Princes. In this way, he claimed to have united both of the rival lines within his own dynasty and created a single, unified English national house. Nearly two centuries later, in 1674, the bodies of two youths were found in construction works at the Tower and were widely (though never conclusively) believed to be the Princes. Charles II had them buried in Westminster Abbey.

Paul Delaroche's "King Edward V and the Duke of York in the Tower of London"

It was during Henry VII's reign in 1485 that the King ordered the foundation of a new military unit specifically associated with the Tower: the Yeomen Warders (popularly called the "Beefeaters"). The Tudors were rulers of breathtaking ambition, letting no earthly power - not even the Pope or the lives of his wives in the case of Henry VIII - stand in the way of their goals. At the same time, they were also innovators of social, political and military policies that helped to forge the centralized English state. One of these many innovations was the creation of a new unit specifically created for guarding the royal houses: the Yeomen. Drawn from the population of freemen ("yeomen") without direct ties to other lesser nobles, the Tudor kings felt they could rely upon this particular unit to protect their own persons. In 1509, when Henry moved out of the Tower of London once peace had settled on the Kingdom, he left a token force of these Yeomen to protect the property, and in effect, he created two of the oldest units in the British military: the Yeomen Warders of the Tower of London and the Yeomen of the Guard, who continued to guard him in his new home. Today, they are the oldest units in the British military and the first permanent standing military force created outside of the system of feudal ties.[20]

---

20 "Yeoman Warders" in the *Historic Royal Palaces: Tower of London* website. Accessed online at: http://www.hrp.org.uk/TowerOfLondon/stories/yeomanwarder

The uniform of Yeomen Warders

There was a growing centralization of other elements of the state as well. One impact on the Tower was the final closure in 1540 of all of the coin mints in the hands of ecclesiastical authorities by Henry VIII, which left the Royal Mint in the Tower as the only source of coins in the realm[21].

However, the reign of the Tudors at the Tower is not primarily remembered for the creation of the Yeoman Warders but instead for its use as the prison for royal women of the era. Four famous women were held here: Anne Boleyn, Lady Jane Grey, Catherine Howard and Elizabeth Tudor (who would become Elizabeth I). All but Elizabeth were executed on the grounds, with Anne and Catherine killed on the orders of Henry VIII. Elizabeth, on the other hand, was not imprisoned until the reign of her sister Mary I, when she was imprisoned in 1554 at the height of

---

21 "Royal Mint Timeline" at the Homepage of the *Museum of the Royal Mint.* Accessed online at: http://www.royalmintmuseum.org.uk/history/timeline/index.html

Wyatt's Rebellion. She was held first in the Tower and then under house arrest for a year until she was released shortly before her sister's death.

Portrait of Anne Boleyn

In addition to Elizabeth, Anne, Jane, and Catherine, Henry VIII also filled the Tower with an unprecedented number of other prisoners, most of whom were unrepentant Catholics. The most prominent of these was Sir Thomas More, the author of *Utopia*, who was imprisoned in the Tower in 1534 while he was Lord Chancellor. More was imprisoned due to his opposition to Protestantism and to the King's marriage to Anne Boleyn, until he was executed in 1535[22].

22 "The Tudors" in the *Historic Royal Palaces: Tower of London* website. Accessed online at:

Portrait of Sir Thomas More

Sir Thomas More's tomb at the Tower of London

The imprisonment of Elizabeth in particular reveals how confinement in the Tower was not always a symbol of royal omnipotence but actually the monarch's frequent impotence. Elizabeth was viewed as a threat to her sister, who sought to marry the Catholic King Phillip of Spain and was widely believed to desire to impose Catholicism upon the nation. Elizabeth was massively popular among the populace, which forced Bloody Mary to act. Mary felt she could not allow her sister the freedom to move about the kingdom after the events of Wyatt's Rebellion, and yet she also feared that killing her sister would spark a much wider rebellion. In her impotence, she took the only (ultimately ineffective) act she could by imprisoning Elizabeth within the Tower.

Bloody Mary

Since its creation, the Tower has sat at the heart of the great events of state. During the reign of Henry VIII (1509 -1547), affairs of the state came to be centered upon one great question: Catholicism or Protestantism. Henry declared England to be independent of the Church in Rome and dissolved all of the monasteries under his dominion. The repercussions of this event have echoed ever since, as it also created the Church of England (often called the "Anglican" or

"Episcopalian" Church). The conflict between Mary and Elizabeth - which in previous generations would have been purely dynastic in nature[23] - had a strongly religious air as well, since those who supported reunification with Rome sided with Mary and those who didn't supported Elizabeth, even as she was locked away in the Tower. With the ascension of Elizabeth, the Protestant faction was solidified in their position and the Arch-Catholic King Philip of Spain was denied his ability to convert England by marrying Mary. All throughout England, and the Tower of London was no exception, fortifications were bolstered and military resources were gathered in anticipation of the coming English invasion which finally occurred in the form of the 1588 Spanish Armada.

Chapter 5: The Tower During the House of Stuart and the English Civil Wars

An 18ᵗʰ century engraving of the Tower of London

Elizabeth I was known as the "Virgin Queen" because she never took a husband nor bore children, so when she died, it was the end of the Tudor line of kings and queens. The Crown instead fell to the House of Stuart, which at that time had been the royal house of Scotland since 1371. As a result, Elizabeth was succeeded by King James I (King James VI of Scotland), the son of Mary, Queen of Scots, who had been briefly imprisoned by Elizabeth I in the Tower between 1569 and 1570 and executed by her in 1587.

James moved to London in 1603, arriving first at the Tower of London, and after his coronation he continued his predecessor's work of strengthening Protestantism in the kingdoms. Perhaps his best known work was when he ordered the translation of the Bible - fittingly named the King James Version - between 1604 and 1611. Naturally, James' continued support of the Church of England led to ongoing resistance during his reign, the most famous event of which

---

23 Like the conflicts between the Lancastrians and Yorkists or between Matilda and Stephen.

was the so-called "Gunpowder Plot" of 1605, when Guy Fawkes and his conspirators attempted to blow up Parliament and kill the King. When Fawkes was captured, he was held and tortured at the Tower before his execution.

Despite that execution, the Tower's history in the early 1600s do show that the monarchy under James I was not rigidly anti-Catholic but instead aimed to walk a fine line of diplomacy between its own Protestantism (and that of many of its subjects) and the powerful Catholic states of mainland Europe, especially Spain. Thus, when the famous Sir Walter Raleigh offended the Catholic King Philip III of Spain with his ceaseless raids on the coast of South America and his search for the golden city of El Dorado, James I bowed to Spanish outrage and had the privateer imprisoned in the Tower several times until his last stint in 1618, after which he was beheaded at Westminster Palace[24].

The tensions and pressures within the religious situation became further complicated when many Protestants began to view the monarchy as "backsliding" towards Catholicism. Some of this may have been inevitable, as the Protestantism that was taking hold among the growing merchant classes of the urban centers (the "Puritans") was strongly Calvinist and rejected ritual, finery and the demonstration of wealth, all of which were central to the early modern monarchy. However, the tension was exacerbated by the second monarch of the House of Stuart: Charles I (reigned from 1626-1649). Charles' falling out with the Puritans began when he attempted to marry a Spanish princess in 1623, and it worsened after his subsequent marriage to a Catholic French princess in 1625. He asserted his right to absolute divine rule and promoted those elements of the Church of England and the Church of Scotland[25] that desired to bring ritual more closely in line with the Catholic faith.

In London, Charles was concerned about the growing unrest throughout his dominions and appointed Colonel Thomas Lunsford Lieutenant of the Tower in 1641. Lunsford was infamous as a murderer and an outlaw yet was loyal to Charles (who had pardoned him) and was considered a vicious and effective commander. Public outcry led to his removal from office four days later, but he served as the commander of the Westminster guard after that and led his soldiers to slaughter protesting citizens of London several times[26]. These and other conflicts with Parliament finally led to the outbreak of the Wars of the Three Kingdoms, of which the English Civil Wars are the best known element.

The King held the Tower via the office of Lieutenant Conyers (who was loyal to him) at the beginning of the civil war, but the strength of the Parliamentarian and Puritan forces in London

---

24 For more or Sir Walter Raleigh's adventures in South America and his search for El Dorado, read *El Dorado: The Search for the Fabled City of Gold* by Jesse Harasta and the Charles River Editors (2014).
25 Two independent Protestant churches both under his nominal control - today often called the Anglican/Episcopalian (Church of England) and Presbyterian (Church of Scotland) churches.
26 "Sir Thomas Lunsford c. 1611-56" at the homepage of the *British Civil Wars, Commonwealth and Protectorate 1638-1660 Project*. Accessed online at: http://bcw-project.org/biography/sir-thomas-lunsford

led to the fall of the Tower in 1643, something they saw as a key element in their defense and control of London. Understanding the importance of the site, the Parliamentarian forces were the first to establish a permanent garrison in the Tower, something which has continued ever since[27]. Overall, the quick capture of the Tower deprived Charles' forces of a crucial strategic advantage and may have contributed significantly to his eventual fall. It also ensured that the Tower was not the site of a prolonged siege during the Civil Wars, and hence the structure suffered relatively little damage in the war as opposed to areas that did see battles, like Glouchester or Bristol. Oliver Cromwell and his New Model Army slowly consolidated control over the three kingdoms of England, Scotland and Ireland after Charles's capture in 1645, and he was executed in 1649.

Under the revolutionary government, the office of Lieutenant of the Tower (by this time the Lieutenants ran the day-to-day operations of the Tower while the Constable office was ceremonial) was retained but given to a radical Puritan and the current Lord Mayor, Isaac Penington, who had zealously attempted to remove what he considered idolatrous images from the churches of London. Penington served on the court that convicted Charles I, but after the restoration of the Monarchy in 1660, he was imprisoned until his death in 1661 in the very same Tower that he had ruled over[28].

During Cromwell's Commonwealth (1649-1661), there were some changes made to the Tower, most notably the fact that the Crown Jewels were removed and melted down and sold. However, in many ways, it remained central to the national administration as a prison for politically powerful enemies, a military stronghold for controlling and protecting London, and a central storehouse for distribution of military supplies throughout the realms. In particular, Cromwell used it to hold those members of the revolutionary movements who called for a reorganization of the social order and wealth to include not simply removing the king but a leveling of wealth (the "Levellers"). For instance, Leveller firebrand writer John Lilburne was held there in 1646 and 1647 in order to stop him from publishing his vitriolic attacks against the hypocrisies of Cromwell's government,[29] as well as his ally Edward Sexby, who rose up against Cromwell in 1653 to demand a more democratic form of government. Sexby was imprisoned in the Tower in 1656 and died of a fever in its walls in 1658[30].

Cromwell's ascension to the king-like status of "Lord Protector" in 1653 alienated many of his more radical followers, and even more turned away from the Commonwealth government after his death in 1658 and the appointment of his unpopular son Richard Cromwell to his position.

---

27 "History of the Tower of London" accessed online at: http://www.ancientfortresses.org/history-of-tower-of-london.htm
28 "Isaac Penington c. 1584 - 61" at the homepage of the *British Civil Wars, Commonwealth and Protectorate 1638-1660 Project*. Accessed online at: http://bcw-project.org/biography/isaac-penington
29 "John Lilburne c. 1615 - 57" at the homepage of the *British Civil Wars, Commonwealth and Protectorate 1638-1660 Project*. Accessed online at: http://bcw-project.org/biography/john-lilburne
30 "Edward Sexby c. 1616 - 58" at the homepage of the *British Civil Wars, Commonwealth and Protectorate 1638-1660 Project*. Accessed online at: http://bcw-project.org/biography/edward-sexby

That move smacked of monarchy, and in 1659, Richard fled into exile and was replaced by a Committee of Safety that dissolved Parliament after the surviving Rump Parliament and the Council of State attempted (and failed) to rule the country in 1659. Governance began to implode, and in 1660, Charles II (Charles I's son) declared himself king. Returning to England, he set up Sir John Robinson as first the Lieutenant and Constable of the Tower in 1660 (continuing until 1679) and then Lord Mayor of London in 1662.

Popular legend holds that the reign of Charles II also marked an important beginning for the folklore of the Tower: the arrival of the ravens. It is certainly possible that ravens had frequented the Tower before this point, as the birds are native to Britain and may have been attracted by the Tower's regular executions and their gruesome habit of eating the eyes of the dead. However, in the centuries after Charles' Restoration, the city grew up around the Tower, and the ravens were extirpated from the surrounding countryside, leaving the Tower's colony as the only remaining ravens among the previous population.

Over time, the legend grew that as long as ravens remained within the Tower, the kingdom - and the monarchy - would not fall, and by the 20th century, this story (which was popularized by the always romantic Victorians) had such appeal that Winston Churchill went about recruiting ravens to replace those killed in the bombs of the Blitz. Since World War II, the British government has recognized the ravens as being enlisted in the military, though some have even been "dismissed" from service after causing particular difficulty for keepers[31]. The Tower takes their birds seriously, and when avian flu threatened the population in 2006, special custom-built indoor aviaries were built on the Tower grounds to isolate them from the disease[32].

---

31 "Myths of the Raven: The Myths and Meanings of the Tower of London Ravens" by Jeffrey Vallance (2007) in *The Fortean Times.* Accessed online at: http://www.forteantimes.com/features/articles/879/myths_of_the_raven.html

32 "Bird Flu Threat Sends Tower of London Ravens Indoors" by the Associated Press 21 Feb 2006 in *Fox News Online.* Accessed online at: http://www.foxnews.com/story/2006/02/21/bird-flu-threat-sends-tower-london-ravens-indoors/

Philippe Kurlapski's picture of one of the Tower's ravens

New threats emerged as the Stuarts reestablished themselves. Spain had been eclipsed as it was exhausted militarily and financially by the century-long, brutal Dutch Revolt (1568-1648), but the victors of those wars, the Dutch Republic, was entering its age of glory: the Dutch Golden Age. The English and Dutch became growing rivals during the late 1660s as each sought to become the premier mercantile power in their overseas empires, and fears of a potential Dutch invasion led the Stuart military to reinvest in the defenses of the Tower of London, including reinforcing its walls against cannonades[33].

---

33 "From Royalty to Artillery" by Robert Wilde. Accessed online at:
   http://europeanhistory.about.com/od/ukandireland/a/prtol4.htm

The Tower was clearly in an era of transition at this point, even though the military roles that it had taken up during the wars and the Commonwealth period remained, including the permanent garrison, the storage of artillery, gunpowder and ammunition, and the administration of the distribution of military supplies throughout the Empire. At the same time, it began to take on some of the earlier, royal roles as well, serving as the home of the royal menagerie, the Yeoman Warders in their Tudor-era regalia, and the storage of royal treasures, especially the Crown Jewels. While the Royal Mint was kept within the Tower, it was completely modernized; in 1662, the new king had screw presses and rolling mills imported for the Mint, removing the hand-striking method that had been used since Roman times[34].

One of Charles II's first acts was to restore the Crown Jewels. While a few items remained intact, such as the Coronation Spoon and the Coronation Chair (which Cromwell sat in when he was invested as Lord Protector), the majority of the items had been broken apart and sold. Restoring the Crown Jewels was seen as necessary for a coronation, and the government spent the princely sum of £12,185 to recreate them[35].

34 "Royal Mint Timeline" at the Homepage of the *Museum of the Royal Mint*. Accessed online at: http://www.royalmintmuseum.org.uk/history/timeline/index.html
35 "The Crown Jewels" at the *Official Website of the British Monarchy*. Accessed online at: http://www.royal.gov.uk/MonarchUK/Symbols/TheCrownJewels.aspx

A replica of St. Edward's Crown

Soon after the Stuart Restoration, the brand new Crown Jewels were once again threatened by a ghost from the Cromwellian past: Colonel Thomas Blood. Born in Ireland in 1618, Blood was originally a soldier for the King in the Civil Wars but switched sides (like many did) when it was obvious that the Monarchy was going to fall. In return, he was made a Justice of Peace and given a large estate. Upon the restoration of Charles II, Blood and his family fled to his native Ireland where, with other deposed Cromwellians, he attempted to capture Dublin Castle and seize the Governor. When that failed, he fled to France, only to make his way back to England and try (again unsuccessfully) to capture the Governor of Ireland in 1670.

The frustrated schemer next turned his attention to the Crown Jewels. The plotter befriended the Keeper of the Jewels and proposed a marriage between his nephew and the Keeper's daughter. During the marriage negotiations, they asked to see the Jewels (already a popular tourist destination) and attacked the Keeper when he opened the door. They hid the Jewels on their persons by flattening the crown with a mallet and tried to shoot their way out of the Tower. They were captured, but, incredibly, they were subsequently pardoned by the King; in fact, Blood lived until 1680 and was a popular figure at Charles' court. He was the last man to steal the Crown Jewels.[36]

---

36 "The Theft of the Crown Jewels" by Ben Johnson. At *Historic UK: The History and Heritage Accommodation Guide*. Accessed online at: http://www.historic-uk.com/HistoryUK/HistoryofEngland/The-Theft-of-the-Crown-Jewels/

Thomas Blood

From Charles II onwards, the Stuarts continued their habit of leaning towards Catholicism and, particularly damning for the increasingly patriotic English, France. Charles II had stayed in France during Cromwell's Commonwealth, and his mother, Henrietta Maria[37], was French Catholic. After Charles's death, his younger brother James took the throne, but his reign was characterized by growing conflict with Parliament, especially over his desire to promote tolerance for Catholics and non-Anglican Protestants. James only ruled for four years (1685-1688), and the final straw was the birth of his son, James Francis Edwards (famed as "The Old Pretender," or to the Jacobites, "The King Over the Water"). Baby James was christened in his

---

37 For whom the colony (and eventual state) of Maryland - a haven for English Catholics - was named.

mother's faith, Roman Catholicism, and things came to a head when the two parties in Parliament (the Tories and Whigs) united and invited Mary - James II's Protestant elder daughter - and her Protestant husband, William of Orange of the Netherlands, to reign. William and Mary[38] arrived at the head of an invading army in what the English remember as "The Glorious Revolution" but which is more infamous in Ireland for its victory in the 1690 Battle of the Boyne. James fled to France and lived there as the "Jacobite" pretender to the throne for the rest of his natural life.

In England, the new royal family consolidated its Protestant control over the kingdom. In the Tower, James' loyal Constable George Legge was replaced by William's loyal man Robert Lucas, the Third Baron Lucas. After the death of William (he was preceded by Mary) in 1702, Mary's younger sister, Queen Anne, took the throne until 1714. She also replaced the Constable upon taking the throne - her favored Montagu Venables-Bertie was made Constable. Like her sister, she bore no children, so upon her death, the Parliament of the United Kingdom sought out her nearest non-Catholic heir: George I of the German House of Hanover.

Chapter 6: The Tower and the British Empire

By the dawn of the 18th century, the Tower's role as a fortification had become largely outdated. The city had sprawled so massively around the Tower that it could no longer effectively defend it, especially the eastern dock regions that stretched far downriver from it. National defense was centered upon the Royal Navy, meaning an enemy that reached the Tower had already fought their way to the heart of the Empire. Likewise, the ability for the Tower to serve as a social control over London had declined alongside the growth of the City, eventually leading to the creation of the Metropolitan Police Force ("Scotland Yard") in 1829 in order to recreate a system of centralized, state-dominated control over the growing metropolis[39].

Thus, it was inevitable that over the course of the 18th and 19th centuries, the Tower was gradually decentralized from the role of administration and maintenance of law and order, and it started to become the more purely symbolic touristic attraction it is today. One element of this was the declining number of prisoners and executions on the site. The final beheading in English history was of Simon Fraser, the Lord Lovat, who was executed on April 9, 1747 after participating in the failed Jacobite Uprising of 1745. The Jacobites, who hailed among the Highland Clans of Scotland, unsuccessfully attempted to overthrow the House of Hanover and return the Stuarts to the throne[40].

That said, the Tower continued to be used for housing prisoners of particular political importance, such as Lord George Gordon, who was imprisoned in 1780 after instigating the

---

38 For whom the College of William and Mary in Virginia was named (they signed the original letters of patent in 1693).

39 "Timeline 1829-1849" at the homepage of the *Metropolitan Police Force*. Accessed online at: http://content.met.police.uk/Site/historicaltimeline

40 "Simon Fraser, Lord Lovat" accessed online at: http://iainthepict.blogspot.com/2011/04/simon-fraser-lord-lovat.html

"Gordon Riots," a massive pro-Catholic street protest. Alongside Gordon, the Tower in 1780 also held Henry Laurens, the former President of the rebellious Continental Congress of the American colonies; Laurens was the only American ever held at the Tower. 1780 was also the last year of hangings at the Tower; after this point, the non-public method of firing squad remained the only form of execution at the Tower.

Henry Laurens

The Tower served admirably in the Napoleonic Wars as the nerve center for the great effort to convert Britain's burgeoning industrial might into military power, with the Tower serving as the primary place where the British gathered war material from across the realm and sent it to battlefields across Europe. After the Wars, the great hero of Waterloo, Arthur Wellesley, the Duke of Wellington, was appointed the Constable of the Tower, by this time considered one of the most prestigious honors given to a member of the British armed forces[41]. Wellesley used his

41 From *The London Gazette* 13 February 1827. Issue 18335 Page 340. Accessed online at:

time as Constable to make some reforms, most notably transforming the Yeoman Warders from an active military unit into a reward for non-commissioned officers with 22 years of exemplary service[42].

The Duke of Wellington

While the development of artillery made the Tower's stone walls obsolete as a military defense (though obviously not obsolete as a prison), it remained a military base and was the headquarters of the Board of Ordnance until 1855. This was no minor role, because in the 19th century, the Board was the second largest government department in the United Kingdom after the Treasury and included a number of roles: manufacturer of gunpowder and armaments, the Royal Military

https://www.thegazette.co.uk/London/issue/18335/page/340
42 "Yeoman Warders" in the *Historic Royal Palaces: Tower of London* website. Accessed online at: http://www.hrp.org.uk/TowerOfLondon/stories/yeomanwarder

Academy, the Royal Engineers and Artillery, the maintenance of fortifications throughout the Empire, the Royal Observatory in Greenwich, the national mapmaking service (the "Ordnance Survey") and many other minor elements of national defense. While some cannons and small arms were stored in the White Tower in this period, the Tower of London was primarily an administrative center for the body. Its closure in 1855 was due to the Board's spectacular failure in provisioning the military in the Crimean War, leading to its dissolution and the incorporation of its elements into the War Office (and from there into the modern Ministry of Defense).

Alongside the Board, much of the crowded space within the Tower was taken up by the Mint. Plans drawn up in 1701 by William Alingham show that the Mint at that point took up all of the space between the inner and outer walls on the three sides not facing the river. The continued growth of the economic might of Great Britain, not to mention the coinage needs of its far-flung colonies, meant that it finally grew out of the limited space within the Tower. Thus, in 1804, work began on a steam-powered facility on nearby Tower Hill (close to where the public beheadings used to take place)[43]. The Tower Hill facility would completely replace the space in the Tower by 1809, where it remained, within sight of the Tower, until its final closure in 1980.

43 "Royal Mint Timeline" at the Homepage of the *Museum of the Royal Mint.* Accessed online at: http://www.royalmintmuseum.org.uk/history/timeline/index.html

Bryan MacKinnon's picture of the scaffolding site for Tower Hill

In 1835, a further major change and a break from over six centuries of tradition occurred when the animals of the menagerie - with the sole exception of the rooks - were moved to the relatively new (1828) London Zoo in Regent's Park. The only animals that remained were the increasingly-famous ravens, whose care was given over to the new position of "Ravenmaster of the Yeoman Warders."

In 1876, the Tower's the Yeoman Warders, the famed "Beefeaters," were further brought into the consciousness of the world through the creation of Beefeater Gin by Burrough's distillery in London. The bottle, then and now, bore an image of the distinctive Beefeater in uniform, and its worldwide distribution has helped to make the Beefeaters famous and turn them into one of the most important attractions of the Tower.[44]

Alongside the administrative purposes, the Tower was increasingly becoming an important destination for visits to the City, particularly because of the presence of the Crown Jewels. The

---

44 "The World's Most Awarded Gin: History" at the *Beefeater Homepage.* Accessed online at:
http://beefeatergin.com/awarded/history

tension between a desire to make these important symbols of the Monarchy available for public admiration and the need to protect them from theft remained. In 1815, a woman reached through the bars protecting the Jewels and attempted to pull the crown through the gap, badly damaging it. She was later found to be legally insane, but additional protections were created, most notably a prohibition on allowing people to touch the objects. The Jewels were further threatened in 1841 when the building next to the Jewel House caught fire. Since the key to the Jewels was inside this building, a police officer wrenched open the protective grate with a crowbar, and the Yeoman Warders were seen carrying the objects by hand through the crowds and into the White Tower[45].

Chapter 7: The Tower's Recent History

The dawn of the 20th century saw more changes to the Tower and to England. The last ruler of the House of Hanover was Queen Victoria (her husband was of the German House Saxe-Coburg and Gotha), and her son, Edward VII, was considered to be the first of his line. The family was of German origin, but in the midst of the passionate anti-German sentiments during World War I, the family changed their name to the House of Windsor.

Under the Windsors, the Tower's role continued to shift. Already, the great administrative departments of the Royal Mint and the Board of Ordnance (not to mention the important but non-administrative Royal Menagerie) had been moved out of the Tower, and the tradition of public executions on Tower Hill had been suspended. Still, the Tower continued as a prison for the first half of the 20th century, and one prominent prisoner of this period was Roger Casement. A diplomat and member of the Foreign Service, Casement had been knighted and recognized for his work in the Belgian Congo and then the Peruvian Amazon, where he laid bare the brutalities and slavery in those countries' rubber industries. He became a public figure in this period, leading an international crusade against such abuses, but in his later years, Casement – an ardent anti-imperialist – joined the struggle for the independence of his native Ireland. He was arrested during the Easter Rebellion for attempting to raise Irish volunteers to fight on the side of Germany for Irish independence and was imprisoned in the Tower for much of 1916, when he was further embroiled in an ugly scandal over the revelations that he was gay. He was hung in Pentonville Prison on the 3rd of August, 1916, and to this day, his name is still remembered in Ireland, the Congo and Peru as a fighter for liberty[46].

---

45 "Visiting the Crown Jewels: A Brief History" at the in the *Historic Royal Palaces: Tower of London* website. Accessed online at: http://www.hrp.org.uk/CrownJewels/Abriefhistory

46 He became particularly well known after Peruvian author Mario Vargas Llosa published *El Sueno del Celta* (The Dream of the Celt) in 2010, a text that was crucial in his receiving the Nobel Prize for Literature that year.

Casement

Many of the later prisoners in the Tower were associated with the military, as it was revived as a military prison during World War II. Rudolf Hess, Adolf Hitler's Depute Fuhrer, was imprisoned there for four days in 1941 after making a secret flight to England to attempt to negotiate a peace treaty. Prominent German spy Josef Jakobs was also held in the Tower in 1941 and, after being found guilty of espionage, was executed at the Tower's practice firing range, which made him the last individual to be put to death at the Tower[47]. The last prisoners to be

47 "Josef Jakobs" at *British Military and Criminal History.* Accessed online at: http://www.stephen-stratford.co.uk/josef_jakobs.htm

held at the Tower were famed East London gangsters Reggie and Ronnie Kray, who had failed to turn up for their National Service (as conscripted soldiers); when their regiment was attached to the Tower, they were held there briefly in 1952[48].

Jakobs

The other remaining administrative role that the Tower continues to fill is the holding place for the Crown Jewels. This ostensibly protective role for the Tower fits well into its growing role as a tourist spot, given that the Jewels are one of the great attractions for the site, and they have only grown in fame over the 20th century as they have increased in value. For instance, in 1910, the Great Star of Africa (the "Cullinan Diamond") was added to the Scepter, and in 1911 the Imperial Crown of India was created to commemorate George V's (the son of Edward VII) visit to India[49].

This remnant of administrative duty aside, today the Tower is almost completely dedicated to serving as a tourist attraction in the heart of London. The Yeoman Warders have become colorfully-dressed tour guides, wearing their Tudor-era dress uniforms as their work costumes. The White Tower is a museum, and there are also displays of coins from the old Royal Mint and an exhibition dedicated to the Royal Menagerie.

Today, the Tower is administered under the Historic Royal Palaces organization, along with several other properties owned by the Queen "in right of Crown," including Hampton Court

48 "Great Misconceptions: Rudolf Hess was the last prisoner kept in the Tower of London" by Justin Pollard. Accessed online at: http://www.historyextra.com/blog/great-misconceptions-0
49 "The Crown Jewels " at the in the *Historic Royal Palaces: Tower of London* website. Accessed online at: http://www.hrp.org.uk/TowerOfLondon/stories/crownjewels

Palace, the Banqueting House, Kensington Palace and Kew Palace. Historic Royal Palaces became an Executive Agency of the Government under the Secretary of State for Culture, Media & Sport in 1989. In 1998, Historic Royal Palaces became a charitable body, although the Tower itself is owned by the Royal Armouries, an independent National Museum under the Crown. Appointed by the Crown, the Royal Constable of the Tower - a position that has existed since the earliest days of the Tower – sits on the Boards of both Historic Royal Palaces and Royal Armouries. The organization is, in essence, an autonomous extension of the Government; four of the seats are directly appointed by the Crown[50] and the other seven by the Secretary of State. [51]

As the Tower has grown in stature as a historic site, its recognition as such has also increased. In 1988, shortly before administration was taken over by Historic Royal Palaces, it was recognized by the United Nations Educational, Scientific and Cultural Organization (UNESCO) as part of its list of World Heritage Sites, a collection of humanity's finest structures[52]. It is also a "Listed" historic structure, giving it Britain's highest level of legal protection. Today it receives around 2.4 million visitors a year, with people coming from across the world to soak up almost 1,000 years of history and ambiance, brutality and beauty, fear and triumph.[53] Certainly, there are few places in the globe that have been so heavily trodden by history and those who made it, including every English king and queen since 1066, writers like Thomas Mallory, Geoffrey Chaucer and Thomas Moore, rebels like Guy Fawkes and Oliver Cromwell, foreign enemies like King John the Good and the Nazi Rudolf Hess, and countless everyday people, soldiers, servants, prisoners and tourists alike.

Bibliography

Allen Brown, Reginald; Curnow, P (1984), Tower of London, Greater London: Department of the Environment Official Handbook, Her Majesty's Stationery Office

Blunt, Wilfred (1976), The Ark in the Park: The Zoo in the Nineteenth Century, Hamish Hamilton, ISBN 0-241-89331-3

Cathcart King, David James (1988), The Castle in England and Wales: an Interpretative History, Croom Helm

Creighton, Oliver (2002), Castles and Landscapes, Continuum

Impey, Edward; Parnell, Geoffrey (2000), The Tower of London: The Official Illustrated

---

50 They are the Director of the Royal Collection, the Keeper of the Privy Purse, the Lord Chamberlain and the Constable of the Tower.
51 "History" at the *Historic Royal Palaces* website. Accessed online at:
http://www.hrp.org.uk/aboutus/whoweare/history
52 "Tower of London" at the homepage of the *UNESCO World Heritage Site List*. Accessed online at:
http://whc.unesco.org/en/list/488
53 "Historic Royal Palaces Annual Review 2010/11" accessed online at:
http://www.hrp.org.uk/Resources/AR_WEB_2011_2.pdf

History, Merrell Publishers in association with Historic Royal Palaces

Jerome, Fiona (2006), Tales from the Tower: Secrets and Stories from a Gory and Glorious Past, Think Publishing

Lapper, Ivan; Parnell, Geoffrey (2000), The Tower of London: A 2000-year History, Osprey Publishing

Liddiard, Robert (2005), Castles in Context: Power, Symbolism and Landscape, 1066 to 1500, Windgather Press Ltd

Parnell, Geoffrey (1993), The Tower of London, Batsford

Sellers, Leonard (1997), Shot in the Tower: The Story of the Spies executed in the Tower of London during the First World War, Leo Cooper

Strickland, Agnes (1840), Lives of the Queens of England from the Norman Conquest. Volume II, Henry Colburn

Wilson, Derek (1998) [1978], The Tower of London: A Thousand Years (2nd ed.), Allison & Busby